TAURUS

—SUN SIGN SERIES—

TAURUS

SUN SIGN SERIES

JOANNA MARTINE WOOLFOLK

TAYLOR TRADE PUBLISHING

LANHAM • NEW YORK • BOULDER • TORONTO • PLYMOUTH, UK

Published by Taylor Trade Publishing
An imprint of The Rowman & Littlefield Publishing Group, Inc.
4501 Forbes Boulevard, Suite 200, Lanham, Maryland 20706
www.rlpgtrade.com

Estover Road, Plymouth PL6 7PY, United Kingdom

Distributed by National Book Network

British Library Cataloguing in Publication Information Available

Library of Congress Cataloging-in-Publication Data

Woolfolk, Joanna Martine.
　Taurus / Joanna Martine Woolfolk.
　　p. cm.—(Sun sign series)
　ISBN 978-1-58979-554-9 (pbk. : alk. paper)—ISBN 978-1-58979-529-7 (electronic)
　1. Taurus (Astrology) I. Title.
　BF1727.2.W66 2011
　133.5'263—dc22　　　　　　　　　　　　　　　　　　　2011003352

∞™　The paper used in this publication meets the minimum requirements of American
National Standard for Information Sciences—Permanence of Paper for Printed Library
Materials, ANSI/NISO Z39.48-1992.

Printed in the United States of America

I dedicate this book to the memory of
William Woolfolk
whose wisdom continues to guide me,

and to
James Sgandurra
who made everything bloom again.

CONTENTS

ABOUT THE AUTHOR

Astrologer Joanna Martine Woolfolk has had a long career as an author, columnist, lecturer, and counselor. She has written the monthly horoscope for numerous magazines in the United States, Europe, and Latin America—among them *Marie Claire*, *Harper's Bazaar*, *Redbook*, *Self*, *YM*, *House Beautiful*, and *StarScroll International*. In addition to the best-selling *The Only Astrology Book You'll Ever Need*, Joanna is the author of *Sexual Astrology*, which has sold over a million copies worldwide, and *Astrology Source*, an interactive CD-ROM.

Joanna is a popular television and radio personality who has been interviewed by Barbara Walters, Regis Philbin, and Sally Jessy Raphael. She has appeared in a regular astrology segment on *New York Today* on NBC-TV and on *The Fairfield Exchange* on

CT Cable Channel 12, and she appears frequently on television and radio shows around the country. You can visit her website at www.joannamartinewoolfolk.com.

ACKNOWLEDGMENTS

Many people contribute to the creation of a book, some with ideas and editorial suggestions, and some unknowingly through their caring and love.

Among those who must know how much they helped is Jed Lyons, the elegant, erudite president of my publishers, the Rowman & Littlefield Publishing Group. Jed gave me the idea for this Sun Sign series, and I am grateful for his faith and encouragement.

Enormous gratitude also to Michael K. Dorr, my literary agent and dear friend, who has believed in me since we first met and continues to be my champion. I thank Michael for his sharp editor's eye and imbuing me with confidence.

Two people who don't know how much they give are my beloved sister and brother, Patricia G. Reynhout and Dr. John T. Galdamez. They sustain me with their unfailing devotion and support.

We are born at a given moment, in a given place,
and like vintage years of wine, we have the
qualities of the year and of the season
in which we are born.

Carl Gustav Jung

INTRODUCTION

When my publishers suggested I write a book devoted solely to Taurus, I was thrilled. I've long wanted to concentrate exclusively on your wonderful sign. You are very special in the zodiac. Astrology teaches that Taurus is the sign of putting down roots and creating beauty and stability. Your sign represents deep devotion, the ability to lavish care on others, and holding fast to one's promises. You're a creator and builder, artist and achiever—linked to all that's fertile and filled with potential to bloom. Karmic teachers say you were specially picked to be a Taurus because in a previous life you taught humanity how to persevere and were a profound source of security. But whether or not one believes in past lives, in *this* life you are Taurus, the great accomplisher.

These days it has become fashionable to be a bit dismissive of Sun signs (the sign that the Sun was in at the time of your birth). Some people sniff that "everyone knows about Sun signs." They say the descriptions are too cookie-cutter, too much a cardboard figure, too inclusive (how can every Taurus be the same?).

Of course every Taurus is not the same! And many of these differences not only are genetic and environmental, but are differences in your *charts*. Another Taurus would not necessarily have your Moon sign, or Venus sign, or Ascendant. However, these are factors to consider later—after you have studied your Sun sign. (In *The Only Astrology Book You'll Ever Need*, I cover in depth differences in charts: different Planets, Houses, Ascendants, etc.)

First and foremost, you are a Taurus. Taurus is the sign the Sun was traveling through at the time of your birth.* The Sun is our most powerful planet. (In astrological terms, the Sun is referred to as a planet even though technically it is a "luminary.") It gives us life, warmth, energy, food. It is the force that sustains us on Earth. The Sun is also the most important and pervasive influence in your horoscope and in many ways determines how others see you. Your Sun sign governs your individuality, your distinctive style, and your drive to fulfill your goals.

Your sign of Taurus symbolizes the role you are given to play in this life. It's as if at the moment of your birth you were pushed onstage into a drama called *This Is My Life*. In this drama, you are the starring actor—and Taurus is the character you play. What aspects of this character are you going to project? (The Taurus loyalty and patience and determination? Your willingness to give your best? Or Taurus's self-indulgence and greedy materialism, its inflexibility and obsessiveness?) Your sign of Taurus describes your journey through this life, for it is your task to evolve into a perfect Taurus.

For each of us, the most interesting, most gripping subject is *self*. The longer I am an astrologer—which at this point is half my lifetime—the more I realize that what we all want to know about is ourselves. "Who am I?" you ask. You want to know what makes you tick, why you have such intense feelings, and whether others

*From our viewpoint here on Earth, the Sun travels around the Earth once each year. Within the space of that year, the Sun moves through all twelve signs of the zodiac, spending approximately one month in each sign.

are also insecure. People ask me questions like "What kind of man should I look for?" "Why am I discontented with my job?" or "The woman I'm dating is a Gemini; will we be happy together?" They ask me if they'll ever find true love and when they will get out of a period of sadness or fear or the heavy burden of problems. They ask about their path in life and how they can find more fulfillment.

So I continue to see that the reason astrology exists is to answer questions about you. Basically, it's all about *you*. Astrology has been described as a stairway leading into your deeper self. It holds out the promise that you do not have to pass through life reacting blindly to experience, that you can within limits direct your own destiny and in the process reach a truer self-understanding.

Astrologically, the place to begin the study of yourself is your Sun sign. In this book, you'll read about your many positive qualities as well as your Taurus issues and negative inclinations. You'll find insights into your power and potentials, advice about love and sex, career guidance, health and diet tips, and information about myriads of objects, places, concepts, and things to which Taurus is attached. You'll also find topics not usually included in other astrology books—such as how Taurus fits in with Chinese astrology and with numerology.

Come with me on this exploration of the "infinite variety" (in Shakespeare's phrase) of being a Taurus.

Joanna Martine Woolfolk
Stamford, Connecticut
June 2011

TAURUS

APRIL 20–MAY 20

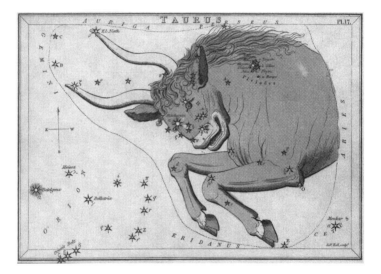

PART ONE

ALL ABOUT YOU

"There is no such thing as great talent without great willpower."

—Honoré de Balzac, novelist, a Taurus

"You simply have to put one foot in front of the other and keep going. Put blinders on and plow right ahead."

—George Lucas, film director, a Taurus

"If you can't stand the heat, get out of the kitchen."

—Harry S. Truman, thirty-third president of the United States, a Taurus

"One of the great signs of security is the ability to just walk away."

—Jack Nicholson, actor, a Taurus

"Love and work are the cornerstones of our humanness."

—Sigmund Freud, founder of modern psychoanalysis, a Taurus

"If you don't know where you're going, you've got to be very careful because you might not get there."

—Yogi Berra, major league baseball player and manager, a Taurus

YOUR TAURUS PERSONALITY

YOUR MOST LIKEABLE TRAIT: Dependability

The bright side of Taurus: Trustworthy, determined, warm, affectionate, artistic

The dark side of Taurus: Obstinate, possessive, rigid, overcautious, a slave to routine

You are steady and enduring, practical and reliable. Determination runs through your character; you have immense capacity for hard work. You are a builder—you put down a foundation and keep constructing. Taurus is the sign of wealth and values, and your driving motivation is to create a life of security. You hold and keep and possess, and you can be controlling and materialistic. Yet your stubbornness and acquisitiveness coexist with a kind and giving nature and an eye for esthetics. Ruled by Venus, you're a sensualist and an artist, blessed with creativity and passionate warmth. Your life lesson is to channel your persistence into worthy endeavors that make a difference in the world. You need to learn the difference between being unyielding and closed off to change—and being committed and devoted.

You are the person others count on in the clutch, the one who perseveres when less determined spirits fall by the wayside. Because perseverance is the quality most needed for success, you tend to be successful.

You are not the pioneer who first strikes out for new territory, but the determined settler who follows and builds houses and towns and cultivates the soil. You go about building the structures in your life in a step-by-step manner, and you have a pronounced stubborn streak. Your willpower is legendary—when you dig in your heels, nothing can budge you. What gives you your greatest strength is your tenacity and steady, relentless drive. You are a purposeful achiever who has endless patience to see a thing through, to make it a success. Your personality has enormous power. You are the original immovable object *and* irresistible force.

Taurus is a Fixed sign, which means its natives are not fond of change. You're set in your ways and simply cannot be rushed into anything new. A different approach creates unease and anxiety. The familiar makes you feel comfortable and secure (fundamental needs), and your attitude might be summed up as "If everything is working fine the way it is, why try something new?" Some of your stubbornness resides in the fact you *know* when you are right. Deep within you a bell sounds when you feel something is wrong, and at that point you will not move. You also like to sift through facts and ponder the contingencies before making up your mind to act. And then, once you're set on your course, nothing can stop you.

Everyone knows you have a temper, although you rarely show it. As a subordinate remarked of a Taurean executive, "No one actually saw him lose his temper, but no one ever doubted that he had one." Generally, you are equable and patient, as patient as time itself, and it is only when opposed (even then, it will take a lot of pushing) that you become angry. Still, there is volcanic activity going on underneath your easygoing, genial exterior. Like a bull quietly grazing in a pasture, you're not looking to challenge anyone, but it would be a fatal mistake for anyone to challenge you.

However, unless someone seriously provokes the fierce side to your personality, you are like Ferdinand the Bull, the gentle cartoon character who loves to sit and smell the flowers. You are caring and affectionate, and you give of yourself. You offer encouragement and advice to nurture and enrich others. If you give your word, you'll fight through Hades itself to keep your promise. Your instinct in relationships is to reach out and say, "I'll be here for you." Once you become a friend, you're a friend forever. In fact, one of your biggest problems in relationships (especially in romantic relationships) is learning when to let go. You're a holder-onto.

This of course is true of you and *things*. You have a great fondness for all things beautiful—and you're never happier than when enhancing the aesthetics of day-to-day life. Ruled by Venus, Goddess of Love and Beauty, you're endowed with genuine creative gifts, responsive to color and design, inspired by art and music. The Taurean taste is supremely elegant, and everything about you (your fashion style, the luxurious feel of your home, etc.) becomes part of your refined, seductive aura. You have a keen eye for what is valuable and are usually an avid collector. It's a rare native of this sign who does not think that possessions, *objets*, wealth, and money are definitely for *having*—and the more the better. Indeed, you were born under one of the two money signs in the zodiac (Cancer is the other one), for Taurus represents prosperity.

People are fascinated by your rare blending of a down-to-earth person who is such a romantic, poetic sort. In Taurus, the stability of an Earth sign combines with the aesthetic influence of Venus to create a responsible, steadfast personality with a deep appreciation for the finer aspects of life. Again and again, you'll find that the unique pairing of your artistic vision with your determination to reach a goal is one of the great secrets to your success.

You are also driven by the search for security—your byword. You look for permanence in career, love, marriage, and home. Let others gad about, jet-set, gallivant, and sleep around. You are happiest at home, surrounded by the beautiful, expensive things you have collected, secure in the warmth of a mate's devotion, steadfast and faithful to those whom you love.

Beneath the surface, you are sensuous and sentimental. You don't give lavish gifts as tokens of affection because you are not a carefree spender—value is what you expect for your hard-earned dollar. (At times, however, you break out and make the extravagant gesture.) You're willing to follow where your heart leads, but find it difficult to display your feelings openly. Your personality is private and self-contained.

Living with you isn't always easy. You can be dogmatic, secretive, stingy, opinionated, and suspicious, and your silent manner may conceal feelings of envy and rivalry. It's hard to get you moving, for you tend to be self-indulgent, even lazy.

You have great stores of energy, however, which you put to use when you want to—not when others want you to.

Your ruling planet, Venus, emphasizes the social side of Taurus. Although basically shy and reserved with strangers, you can be a wonderful host or hostess. You like to entertain those you are fond of. You may not indulge as freely in frivolous pleasures as, say, Leo or Libra natives, but you are renowned for enjoying good food and good wine in plush surroundings. You believe in pampering yourself with the comforts of the good life.

As a person born under this sign, you are an endearing combination of the dependable and sensible, the sensitive and emotional. Inside every practical, stolid-seeming Taurean, there is a romantic dreamer struggling to get out.

THE INNER YOU

You need order in your life—you become anxious when things are out of control. And because the unfamiliar makes you feel insecure, you tend to cut yourself off from fresh experiences. You need to be more open to change. Having beautiful things is important to you, and your instinct for collecting even spills over into relationships. You hold fast to those you care about. You have a few close friends rather than many casual acquaintances. In love, you're happiest when involved in a caring, committed relationship. The other side of the coin is you will stay too long in an unhappy love affair or marriage, which is doubly painful in your case because you are deeply sensitive. A rebuff or harsh word is very upsetting to you—and with strangers you often feel self-conscious.

HOW OTHERS SEE YOU

You're thought of as a serene influence, someone to depend on, and you're admired for your organized mind. Not many people realize that you're sensitive and easily wounded. You are trusted as a tastemaker, and your artistic and aesthetic opinion is welcomed. Because you have sound instincts about money, your financial advice is also sought. On the other hand, people resent your tendency to be dogmatic. Even if you're right, others don't understand why you have to be so unyielding.

GUARD AGAINST: Becoming Stuck

Your strength lies in your fixity of purpose, but you have a great propensity for getting bogged down. Your concentrated focus can turn into inflexibility and becoming entrenched in place. Taurus is a sign that can grow roots that are immovable. Your shadow side is someone rigid, narrow, and trapped by the superficial.

At issue is your need for security. You want permanence and fixity. You are habit-bound; habits give your life order. You're resistant to change because it may mean losing something you value. You oppose anything that threatens what you want to preserve—whether this is simply a familiar routine or the entire structure of how you live.

When you fight against change people see you as pigheaded and unteachably stubborn. You won't alter an opinion and will say no to any new suggestion. You retreat into old thinking patterns and fixate on maintaining the status quo. Even if you know change is necessary—and inevitable—you'll dig in your heels, procrastinate until the decision time is past, and let what's familiar dictate your life.

But being stable and being stuck are two different things. Stability gives a solid foundation upon which to expand; being stuck is totally limiting. Stability has a growing quality to it; being stuck has resistance. These are subtle differences but they're crucial to your quality of life. If you're not continuing to learn, then you're at a dead end.

Taurus is the sign of spring, the season of growing and renewal. Your Taurus staying power allows you to create, but you must also allow the coming to fruition to unfold. You must not hold onto the things (habits, emotional situations) that impede new growth. Just as the seasons change, life changes, and your Taurus ability to commit to a creation means you can make something glorious bloom. Your journey is to discover how to embrace positive change and make the most of it.

YOUR GREATEST CHALLENGE:
Learning How Valuable You Are

Taurus is the sign of money, wealth, value, and self-value, but too often the value you put on self is tied to the material. What you deem to be worthy is projected outward by money and things rather than inward on yourself. You define yourself by what you *have* rather than who you *are*. You care what people think of you, and if you possess the outer trappings (nice clothes, expensive things) you feel you gain the respect and admiration of others.

Inwardly, actually, you're shy and tend to be painfully self-conscious—usually the result of a poor self-image during childhood. Many Taureans had solitary childhoods, spending long hours entertaining themselves alone or experiencing difficulty being accepted by cliques in school. New people and new situations create anxiety because these are unknown quantities. You feel safest with the known and familiar and with people you know care for you.

As a Taurus, you suffer from secret fears—fear of making a mistake, of being judged inferior, of not having, of abandonment, of taking a risk. You'll stay with what you know rather than losing on the unknown.

These inner insecurities add to your desire for financial wherewithal and beautiful possessions. With these, you will be safe, important, acclaimed by others, and fulfilled. You will be valued. But your greatest challenge, Taurus, is to discover your true value—*who* you are. You were born with amazing creativity and intelligence; you put real craftsmanship into your work. You're superior in your self-discipline and have the perseverance to make whatever you focus on permanent. You are also exceedingly rare in your power to love and be a force for good in the world.

YOUR ALTER EGO

Astrology gives us many tools in our lives to help manage our struggles and solve problems. One of these tools is to reach into your opposite sign in the zodiac—your "polarity." For you, Taurus, this is Scorpio, sign of transition and transformation. Scorpio has esoteric symbolism, for this sign represents moving through "death-like" endings (e.g., endings to relationships or a chosen career) and rebirthing into a new beginning. Scorpio has an amazing capacity to keep on keeping on. Life crises that might make other people take to their beds for a month curled up in a fetal position are what Scorpio characterizes as "It is what it is."

Taurus and Scorpio both have in common the quality of stubbornness. You, Taurus, are stubborn about a habit, a way of thinking, a pattern of behavior. But Scorpio is stubborn about its very survival through any situation, no matter what those circumstances are. Astrology teaches that Scorpio's stoicism is the tool through which it learns life lessons—and that Scorpio is destined to undergo some kind of critical "death" experience that transforms it into someone of deeper wisdom and love. In Charles Dickens's beloved novel *A Christmas Carol*, the character of Ebenezer Scrooge passes through a Scorpio experience that transforms him forever afterwards into a man who "truly knew how to keep Christmas." The Scorpio rebirthing process always brings the person to an emotional and spiritual awakening.

Taurus, you can access this power. Especially when you're feeling most stuck and most despairing of ever getting out of your cage, you can take control, face "what is," and make your leap over the moat for freedom. It's not in your nature to cut and run, but you can do this when your psychic survival is at stake. You have profound capacity to move out of the darkness and find the light that allows new blooming. Taurus is the sign of spring and new growth—growth that always comes after a winter of deadness. When you're in a situation of cold desolation, reach into your opposite sign's ability not only to move through change but to *create* it. You have extraordinary strength of character, Taurus, and you possess deep wisdom about what's most valuable to you. Combine this with the Scorpio courage to reinvent, and you will certainly transform into a force of nature.

In turn Scorpio has much to learn from you—among the most priceless is your generosity of heart. You have an abundantly affectionate nature that reaches out to form warm connections. Scorpio has difficulty making emotional contact. It tends to be suspicious and become very isolated. Scorpio has a way of holding on to pain, and can carry around dark anger. Scorpio can learn from you that to love others is to carry around joy. Even by tapping into your Taurus appreciation of beauty, Scorpio can bring pleasure and artistic expression into its life.

TAURUS IN LOVE

Taurus is an earthy, voluptuous sign with an idealistic take on love. Since you're a Venus-ruled sign with a great appreciation for beauty, you're drawn to people with physical attractiveness—although good looks and superficial appearances are certainly not enough. Your deepest desire is to be in loving partnership with someone you can trust and depend on, and share confidences with, someone who will be your helpmate through thick and thin.

At the same time, you have an abundantly affectionate, erotic physicality. Your indolent, sybaritic sensuality is lit with inner fire. To paraphrase a line from the movie *Working Girl*, you have a heart made for romance and a body made for sin. For you to get the attention of someone you're attracted to, all you have to do is beam your erotic antenna in that person's direction. You're skilled in the art of seduction.

However, when it comes to falling in love, you are cautious. If you're a Taurus woman, you're certainly not a lady for a day, or even for a weekend. Your need is for security and stability, and casual is not a word in your vocabulary of love. A man must court you and make you feel secure. When you're confident about the relationship, you're warm, enticing, very affectionate and demonstrative—and your sexual appetite is hearty.

If you're a Taurus man, you look over the field before you decide. You want a woman who will satisfy you for the long haul. This is not to say you'll turn down an invitation to a weekend frolic with a sexy babe. You've had your share of one-night stands, and you're a skilled and erotic lover. But if a woman scratches the surface of your persona, she'll discover a man who doesn't want a *relationship* unless he thinks it's going to last.

Sexually, whether you're a Taurus man or a Taurus woman, you have great stores of passion to give. Generally, your early sexual experiences are with someone older who can teach you not only erotic pleasure, but the delights of fine food and wines, art and music. You're demanding sexually and lusty in bed, but you're also bountifully generous. You never withhold caresses and affection, and you enjoy a romantic, elegant setting for lovemaking—candlelight and silky sheets are part of the ambiance. You want to feel idolized by a lover.

Basically, you want someone you feel can take care of you—in the sense of being totally in your corner and a great supporter. You want a relationship in which the two of you immerse yourselves in the sexuality of your bodies and the profundity of your emotions. Your relationship also thrives on little romantic touches (such as giving each other silly sentimental gifts) and lots of passionate lovemaking.

With your capacity for love and faithfulness—and for giving sexual affection—it would seem a relationship with you is the perfect one. But the underside of loyalty and focused passion is possessiveness and jealousy. You don't give your lover enough space and feel threatened if he or she wants time away from you.

You tend to view your lover as something you own, and your protectiveness turns controlling. Taurus is also habit-bound, and the relationship can become claustrophobic. Even if *you're* the one who is unhappy, you'll stay bound into an adversarial partnership, hoping things will get better—determined you're not going to "fail." At the start of a relationship, sex and money are a huge drawing power, and too often you find out later you made a mistake by succumbing to these early draws.

However, for the person who can return to you in kind the loyalty and affection you offer, and also give you the emotional security you need, having your committed Taurus love is a wonderful treasure.

TIPS FOR THOSE WHO WANT TO ATTRACT TAURUS

Taureans are not going to be rushed. They like everything, including a friendship or a love affair, to be built on a firm foundation. That may require restraint and patience, but these are qualities Taureans appreciate, for they possess those traits themselves.

Hint: The first move is up to you. Taurus is slow to make up his or her mind, and the opportunity will be gone if you don't seize the initiative.

Show them you like to be in their company, and try to amuse them. These quiet, easygoing people respond to those from whom they can borrow laughter. You'll find them charming companions, interested and interesting. A tendency to be somewhat ponderous or go on at excessive length can be corrected with an apt remark at the right time.

If you tell a joke, remember that Taurus's sense of humor tends to be broad, robust, Rabelaisian. Physical jokes strike their funny bones.

If you're feeding a Taurus, feed him or her well. Take her to a restaurant where the chef knows his business and where you can get a good bottle of wine. Cook him a meal at home that shows you know your way around a kitchen, and don't skimp on the portions.

If the conversation starts to lag, try that never-failing topic of interest: money. By all means, show off your prized possessions, from stamps to porcelain miniatures to jade, or even Indian Head pennies. To a Taurean, it's all endlessly fascinating.

Don't monopolize the conversation. Once Taureans get started, they like to talk. And don't be niggardly with praise—for their home, their car, clothes, jewelry, their just plain good taste, and, above all, for them.

TAURUS'S EROGENOUS ZONES:
Tips for Those with a Taurus Lover

Our bodies are very sensitive to the touch of another human being. The special language of touching is understood on a level more basic than speech. Each sign is linked to certain zones and areas of the body that are especially receptive and can receive sexual messages through touch. Many books and manuals have been written about lovemaking, but few pay attention to the unique knowledge of erogenous zones supplied by astrology. You can use astrology to become a better, more sensitive lover.

For Taurus, the special body area is the throat and neck, and light touching, kissing, and fondling of this zone will quickly raise a Taurean's sexual temperature. When fixing a Taurus man's tie, lightly glide your fingernails over his throat. Brush the back of a Taurus woman's neck in an affectionate gesture. Both men and women enjoy kisses and gentle bites on the back of the neck and the throat.

Here is a massage technique that will surely please: (1) While Taurus lies on his or her back, gently vibrate the area under the earlobes with your fingertips, using little circular motions. Trace a path down to the collarbone. Repeat until the entire front of the neck has been massaged. (Be very gentle around the windpipe.) (2) Taurus likes to lie on his or her stomach while you trace vertical paths from the hairline to the top of the spine, using your fingertips to vibrate the flesh and muscles.

This technique will thoroughly relax Taurus and make him or her very receptive to lovemaking.

TAURUS'S AMOROUS COMBINATIONS: YOUR LOVE PARTNERS

TAURUS AND ARIES

Right away your elegance and social grace and Aries's flashy extroversion make a sparkling combination, which intrigues you both. You're not as quick on the trigger as Aries (emotionally or physically), but you both do have a mutual interest in making love. Aries is expressive and you are sensual, and you're bound to have fun while the affair lasts. In time, though, your possessiveness will strike angry sparks from fiery Aries. You'll also argue about money—you tend to be careful and conservative, whereas Aries is reckless and a spendthrift. Aries's impulsiveness in making decisions annoys Fixed Taurus, who dislikes a sudden change in routine. Neither of you is able to adjust to what the other needs emotionally. An affectionate affair can turn into a difficult marriage.

TAURUS AND TAURUS

This is not the most exciting union ever, for you're both domestic creatures who prefer safety to adventure. This doesn't bother you, though, because you are committed types who want to take the time to make sure love and trust will last in the relationship. Both share a fondness for money and are hardworking, loyal, and affectionate. A Taurus woman tends to be more sentimental than a Taurus man, but each is as possessive as the other, which works out fine. You two are earthy and direct about sexual needs and find deep physical gratification together. The only trouble in paradise is that boredom is the long-term threat. The perfect solution is for each of you to develop some outside hobbies and friends without raising the possessive hackles of the other.

TAURUS AND GEMINI

You and Gemini are completely unalike in temperament. Taurus is stolid, fixed in opinions, resistant to change. Gemini is flighty, restless, vacillating. But you may find each other intriguing for that very reason—for a little while. Gemini has an interesting intelligence and makes you laugh. In turn, Gemini is attracted to your passions and becomes immersed in your deep sensuality. But all too soon your instinct for security and stability will be offended by volatile Gemini. You are too much a creature of habit to go along with Gemini's constant need for new stimulation. Gemini interprets demands for affection and constancy as restrictions—and eventually, your requests for closeness are simply too much for Gemini, who seeks escape.

TAURUS AND CANCER

You have a lot going for you. You're both home-lovers, sentimentalists, and highly sexed. You're both able to be intimate on many levels, certainly physically, but also emotionally and intellectually. Each of you is creative, and the pursuits you like mesh well (such as cooking, decorating, collecting). Also, Taurus's placid, easygoing nature is a good antidote for Cancer's moodiness—although because you're plainspoken and upfront, you have to be careful not to slight Cancer's feelings. Cancer needs someone strong like you to depend on; in turn, Cancer gives you the loyalty and feedback you need. Your Taurus bent is to be ambitious for money and security, and Cancer has exactly these same goals. Similar interests and desires make for a harmonious mating.

TAURUS AND LEO

Leo demands constant praise and adulation and is forever competing with you. As a result, you dig in your heels and get more sullen with each passing day. Taurus needs appreciation and Leo needs worship, but neither will get what you need from the other. In addition, Leo is extravagant, whereas you hold tightly to the dollar—you want to get your money's worth. There's also a basic conflict between your desire for a well-ordered schedule and Leo's need for a larger-than-life existence. Taurus and Leo are both Fixed signs, which means both of you are loyal (a good thing), but each is also stubborn and won't give an inch when crossed. With you two, this happens often. Sexually, you're well matched, but Leo thinks life is a circus and tries to perform in all three rings at once. You find this hard to take, or even to watch.

TAURUS AND VIRGO

It's love at first sight. Both of you are homebodies and share the same intellectual pursuits. You have good vibes not only as a romantic couple but as a business partnership—your Taurus tenacity and Virgo's sharp mind are a winning combination for success as a team. And you keep a careful eye on expenditures, which pleases thrifty Virgo. Although the two of you lack what might be called a spontaneous approach to life, neither of you puts a high value on that. Each of you wants stability and to feel your lives have purpose. You may have to work at adjusting to each other sexually, for Taurus is more physical and sensual than Virgo. However, you'll probably waken Virgo's sleeping passions. And the two of you have everything else in common.

TAURUS AND LIBRA

You find Libra a warm, romantic, vibrant partner. Libra was born to charm and titillate, and your steady ways balance Libra's indecisiveness. However, money is a problem because it's a two-edged sword. What you have in common is that you both tend to be acquisitive and like to collect beautiful things. However, you'll discover Libra is a spendthrift and certainly doesn't share your reverential attitude toward a dollar. Both of you are ruled by Venus and have sensual natures, but each expresses this quality differently. A difficulty is that Libra is more in love with *love* than with you. In time, Libra's fickleness and casual air can drive you wild, and Libra will certainly resent your possessiveness. This romantic pairing may not last long.

TAURUS AND SCORPIO

You and Scorpio are opposite in the zodiac, but you have more in common than other opposites. You're both determined and ambitious, both need to feel safe, and neither is much of a rover. However, two strong wills are at work here. Your single-mindedness is focused on creating security, whereas Scorpio's is on creating change. Almost immediately, you two lock horns over control issues. You're too much alike in your stubbornness and inflexibility. Where you do mesh is sexually. Your passionate eroticism meets more than its match in Scorpio—in fact, the sexual element in your affair borders on the obsessive. But Scorpio's overbearing, possessive, jealous nature makes you simmer with resentment. This is a tempestuous affair, and neither of you has the tolerance to make the union last.

TAURUS AND SAGITTARIUS

This might work if you can tie a string to Sagittarius's kite and hold on tight. You're attracted to each other physically, for your Taurus passions are ignited by Sagittarius's uninhibited lovemaking. But you find it difficult to deal with Sagittarius's roving eye and search for novelty. Sagittarius thinks he or she should have freedom to explore life and looks on responsibilities and commitments as heavy anchors. Therefore, Sagittarius has an easy, live-and-let-live attitude about sex and everything else, whereas you are serious and (the kiss of death with Sagittarius) possessive. Sagittarius refuses to stay under someone else's thumb. No dull moments, but a good deal of quarreling. At your cores, you're too different, though an affair might be fun.

TAURUS AND CAPRICORN

Capricorn is a strong match for you. Both of you have passions that are straightforward and uncomplicated, and neither is a fly-by-night who can't deal with responsibility. Quite possibly your relationship won't be infused with a whole lot of romance, but you will enjoy plenty of healthy sex. You find communion of spirit and an expression of love in your deep eroticism. You two also share the same goals and like the same kinds of friends. You're both fond of security and money and, happily, make each other feel safe financially. Capricorn is a bit more secretive than you'd like, but all the same, Capricorn's loyalty makes you secure. And you're charmed by Capricorn's unexpected sense of humor. Auguries for the long term are promising.

TAURUS AND AQUARIUS

Astrologically, Taurus and Aquarius are Fixed signs, but each shows fixity very differently. You're security-minded and pride yourself on your determination and practicality. Aquarius is fixed in its insistence on individuality and therefore far more uncon-ventional in lifestyle. Neither is likely to approve of the other.

You're conservative, careful, and private, whereas Aquarius is avant-garde and outgoing. You're also lusty and passionate, while Aquarius operates on a mental plane. Aquarius looks for openness and self-expression in a relationship, while you need security and comfort. You want to have and to hold, which Aquarius interprets as confining. Aquarius—a fancy-free loner who resents ties that bind—sooner or later slips away.

TAURUS AND PISCES

Pisces may not altogether understand your practical, materialistic approach to life. But your dependability supplies the anchor Pisces needs to keep from drifting away into a private sea of fantasy. You're hardworking and responsible, and you set a good example for Pisces, who can be somewhat of a lazy dilettante. Also, your steady, easygoing nature helps Pisces through its frequent changes of mood. Though Pisces can be a bit fey for you, sexually you're well suited. Pisces wants to please and enchant and brings an imaginative approach to lovemaking. Taurus's passion and Pisces's sensuality make a divinely romantic coupling. The real glue in your relationship is loyalty; you two are at your best in demonstrating love and protectiveness. You're devoted, and Pisces is adoring.

YOUR TAURUS CAREER PATH

Your sign of Taurus is the money sign of the zodiac—the sign of wealth, possessions, ownership, and values. Taurus represents material belongings and the search for financial security. Pursuing a career is as natural to you as breathing. You have a desire to achieve—but more than this, a desire for your achievements to bring you a sense of security. Even when you were growing up, you may have opened a savings account and were eager to earn extra money through odd jobs after school or weekends. Taurus has an instinct for where the money is—the possibilities of a new project, the chances of an idea being lucrative—and no one is better at saving, collecting, and putting away for a rainy day.

Yet it isn't merely squirreling away that interests you (though you'll do this in lean times). Taurus is a Venus-ruled sign, which means you're extremely creative. You may have an actual artistic bent and be drawn to the world of an artist, writer, performer, or craftsperson. Or you may use your creativity in what might be called pure business. You may operate in the arena of banking, finance or commerce, but you'll think up new ways of doing business and use your imagination to expand your product or service to a wider public.

Your quest in your work is to utilize your artistic taste to create something permanent, important, aesthetically elegant, and that provides a source of wealth. Your career may be inventive, explorative and on the cutting edge, but to be seen as unusual or unique is not the purpose of your work. The purpose of your career is to *gain*.

Astrologically, Taurus is known as the Builder. Your cosmic role is to set a foundation into place and construct a castle. You don't waste time building a hovel—you strive for something far more impressive. In a career, therefore, you're drawn to large-scale work (e.g., careers in architecture, real estate development, landscape design, commercial art, antiques). You're good at gardening, cooking, restaurant and hotel professions, or work in fashion, jewelry, and cosmetics. You enjoy displaying your talents and the fine possessions you accumulate. You don't hide your light. Because you're comfortable being seen by others, you're often in the limelight in business and the arts. Certainly, with your good head for money, banking, financial investment, and the stock market are lucrative for you.

With your fondness for acquisition, however, you need to be careful not to get bogged down in materialism. A danger is becoming owned by what you own. Investing *things* with the power to give you importance and status leads to a very shallow existence. It also promotes judging others by superficial trappings. With colleagues, contacts, and clients, you may start to size up people's "worth" by how they look and dress and how much they're paid. When your work becomes your sole means of establishing a sense of power, you can turn negative—crabbed, demanding, mean-spirited, and a bully.

Still, Taurus has the capacity to move past a base desire for accumulation and power, to move past the superficial. You can create a benign kingdom that brings worth to the world. In your career, you have a knack for dealing with others and a charmingly subtle way of guiding them in a positive direction. One of your strong points is organization. You can handle detail and set about a task step-by-step. You're intensely practical and don't waste time or talent on vague, unworkable ideas. And in whatever you undertake, you do so with patience and tenacity. In short, you usually rise to the top of your profession because you're a prodigious worker, a commonsense thinker, and a talented manager of people—and most of all because your dedication and commitment come from the heart.

TAURUS AND HEALTH:
ADVICE FROM ASTROLOGY

Movement is your key to well-being. Taurus is the sign that can get most stuck in place—mentally, emotionally, and certainly physically. Putting on excess weight will always be a problem, for you enjoy good food and love desserts. You also have a tendency to be inactive, for you like to indulge yourself in comfort rather than exercise. You must push yourself because, with indolence and too much poundage, you'll slide into emotional despondency. Even a ten-minute walk every day will work wonders. Try dancing or dance-exercise; Taurus is an artistic sign, drawn to music, and exercise you do to music is greatly beneficial to your mind, body, and spirit. Taurus rules the throat and neck, and you are prone to colds and sore throats. Make sure your neck is warm, eat sensibly, and keep moving. You have amazingly strong health!

Advice and useful tips about health are among the most important kinds of information that astrology provides. Health and well-being are of paramount concern to human beings. Love, money, or career takes second place, for without good health we cannot enjoy anything in life.

Astrology and medicine have had a long marriage. Hippocrates (born around 460 B.C.), the Greek philosopher and physician who is considered the father of medicine, said, "A physician without a knowledge of astrology has no right to call himself a physician." Indeed, up until the eighteenth century, the study of astrology and its relationship to the body was very much a part of a doctor's training. When a patient became ill, a chart was immediately drawn up. This guided the doctor in both diagnosis and treatment, for the chart would tell when the crisis would come and what medicine would help. Of course, modern Western doctors no longer use astrology to treat illness. However, astrology can still be a useful tool in helping to understand and maintain our physical well-being.

THE PART OF YOUR BODY RULED BY TAURUS

Each sign of the zodiac rules or governs a specific part of the body. These associations date back to the beginning of astrology. Curiously, the part of the body that a sign rules is in some ways the strongest and in other ways the weakest area for natives of that sign.

Your sign of Taurus rules the throat and neck, which includes the vocal cords, palate, and tonsils. Generally, Taureans have long, expressive necks, and women of this sign have lovely skin around the throat and collarbone area. Both genders are known for having melodious speaking voices, and many are fine singers. Taurus taste buds are keen, and generally all natives of this sign enjoy good food. Indeed, your tendency to put on weight grows more pronounced as you get older—and though this is true of everyone, you above all need to be vigilant.

You're particularly vulnerable to colds, coughs, sore throats, laryngitis, swollen glands, stiff necks, and minor injuries around the neck. When exposed to wintry wind and cold weather, you should take care to bundle up with scarves and mufflers. As a Taurus, you're also subject to tonsillitis and earaches. Colds seem to settle into your throat, and aren't easily shaken off. When you get physically tired or overly tense, you tend to get coughs and stiff necks. Many Taureans go through life with a semipermanent "crick" in their necks.

Your sign of Taurus also rules the thyroid gland, which can cause serious weight problems if it is malfunctioning. In addition, your ruling planet, Venus, has an effect on the parathyroids, which control calcium levels in the body. Traditionally, Venus also rules the throat, kidneys, and lumbar region. Being Venus-ruled, you sometimes suffer from back strain, especially because you tend to be sedentary.

DIET AND HEALTH TIPS FOR TAURUS

A diet low in fat, sugar, and starch is particularly important because you need to fight the battle of the bulge. You're likely to eat fattening foods, to be sluggish and indolent, and to dislike exercise. You may suffer from puffy eyes and jowls, and Taureans' faces are apt to get heavier as time goes by. Moderate exercise and good diet should be a strict discipline in your life.

Taurus's cell salt* is sulphate of sodium, a mineral that controls the amount of water in the system. It is present in the liver and

---

*Cell salts (also known as *tissue salts*) are mineral compounds found in human tissue cells. These minerals are the only substances our cells cannot produce by themselves. The life of cells is relatively short, and the creation of new cells depends on the presence of these minerals.

pancreas, and in the hormones of the kidneys. An imbalance of this mineral can cause bloating, symptoms of congestion around the thyroid gland, and a feeling of being waterlogged. Foods that contain this mineral that you need are asparagus, beets, spinach, horseradish, Swiss chard, cauliflower, cucumber, onions, pumpkin, cranberries, and raw nuts. Celery can help you to clear your system after overindulgence. Carbohydrates have a way of turning into fat in your body and should be eaten in limited portions. You have trouble digesting heavy, rich foods.

To keep your thyroid functioning at its best, eat food with natural iodine, such as fish and seafood. Other foods that keep you healthy are eggs, liver, kidney beans, wheat germ, fresh fruit, and green salads. Drink plenty of water to keep your system flushed out.

In general, you should coddle your throat, try not to catch colds, wear warm head-and-neck coverings in winter, and keep foreign objects out of your ears. Stretching exercises for the neck are very beneficial. Walking is a superb activity for you, and you're an especially good candidate for dance-exercise. You have grace and artistry, and are fond of music—dancing won't even feel like exercise.

THE DECANATES AND CUSPS OF TAURUS

Decanate and *cusp* are astrological terms that subdivide your Sun sign. These subdivisions further define and emphasize certain qualities and character traits of your Sun sign Taurus.

WHAT IS A DECANATE?

Each astrological sign is divided into three parts, and each part is called a *decanate* or a *decan* (the terms are used interchangeably).

The word comes from the Greek word *dekanoi*, meaning "ten days apart." The Greeks took their word from the Egyptians, who divided their year into 360 days.* The Egyptian year had twelve months of thirty days each, and each month was further divided into three sections of ten days each. It was these ten-day sections the Greeks called *dekanoi*.

---

*The Egyptians soon found out that a 360-day year was inaccurate and so added on five extra days. These were feast days and holidays, and not counted as real days.

Astrology still divides the zodiac into decanates. There are twelve signs in the zodiac, and each sign is divided into three decanates. You might picture each decanate as a room. You were born in the sign of Taurus, which consists of three rooms (decanates). Which room of Taurus were you born in?

The zodiac is a 360-degree circle. Each decanate is ten degrees of that circle, or about ten days long, since the Sun moves through the zodiac at approximately the rate of one degree per day. (This is not exact because not all of our months contain thirty days.)

The decanate of a sign does not change the basic characteristics of that sign, but it does refine and individualize the sign's general characteristics. If you were born, say, in the second decanate of Taurus, it does not change the fact you are Taurus. It does indicate that you have somewhat different and special characteristics from those Taurus people born in the first decanate or the third decanate.

Finally, each decanate has a specific planetary ruler, sometimes called a subruler because it does not usurp the overall rulership of your sign. The subruler can only enhance, or add to, the distinct characteristics of your decanate. For example, your entire sign of Taurus is ruled by Venus, but the second decanate of Taurus is subruled by Mercury. The influence of Mercury, the subruler, combines with the overall authority of Venus to make the second decanate of Taurus unlike any other in the zodiac.

FIRST DECANATE OF TAURUS

April 20 through April 30
Keyword: Acquisition
Constellation: Triangulum, the Triangle, mystic symbol of truth and harmony.
Planetary Subruler: Venus

Venus is both your ruler and subruler, and its gracious influence is prominent in your character. Though you have strong likes and dislikes, you are not abrasive about them. You have a charming social touch, and many friends are devoted to you. Your kind and sympathetic nature is easily imposed on. You have an artistic eye for beauty and design and may possess musical ability. Venus in this decanate indicates a love of beautiful possessions. Generally, your instinct for value is useful; in time, many of your possessions should be worth more than you paid for them. Sometimes, however, you are too money-oriented and acquisitive. The double-influence of Venus encourages both greediness and indolence, and you must concentrate on self-discipline (which you have stores of!) in order to stay in balance.

SECOND DECANATE OF TAURUS

May 1 through May 10
Keyword: Evaluation
Constellation: Eridanus, the River Po, a winding current that symbolizes justice.
Planetary Subruler: Mercury

Mercury combines with Venus (Taurus's ruler) to give you an inquisitive mind and a great talent for organization. You are conservative in approach, but also possess intuitive powers that you should use more often. In particular, creative ideas often pop into your head. Because you are a determined worker, you inspire trust on the part of others. You have an instinct for cooperation, but you also need the freedom to set your own pace, away from distractions. Your mental powers are very strong, and you can take complex ideas and make them understandable to others. You're an excellent teacher and adviser. Mercury here bestows an ability to speak and write effectively, even eloquently. Sometimes you meddle too much into other people's affairs, and you have a tendency to forget small details.

THIRD DECANATE OF TAURUS

May 11 through May 20
Keyword: Determination
Constellation: Perseus, the Rescuer, the hero with winged feet and a sword who slew the Gorgon Medusa. Perseus is symbolic of victory.
Planetary Subruler: Saturn

The meditative qualities of Saturn combine with harmonious Venus to give you quiet determination and strength of character. People think of you as stable and reliable, for you are not easily deterred once you're set on a goal. You possess an active mind and are keenly observant. Usually you deal with problems by thoroughly analyzing them before you act. You are not wishy-washy about letting others know where you stand; you'd rather confront a difficulty than evade and worry about it. You have strong, deep feelings, and in romantic relationships are loyal and protective and an emotional nurturer. You can easily become the sacrificer. A fault is that you tend to be too serious. Sometimes you are hurt by what others say because you take things too much to heart.

WHAT IS A CUSP

A cusp is the point at which a new astrological sign begins.* Thus, the cusp of Taurus means the point at which Taurus begins. (The word comes from the Latin word *cuspis*, meaning "point.")

When someone speaks of being "born on the cusp," that person is referring to a birth time at or near the beginning or the end of an astrological sign. For example, if you were born on May 20, you were born on the cusp of Gemini, the sign that begins on May 21. Indeed, depending on what year you were born, your birth time might even be in the first degree of Gemini. People born on the very day a sign begins or ends are often confused about what sign they really are—a confusion made more complicated by the fact that the Sun does not move into or out of a sign at *exactly* the same moment (or even day) each year. There are slight time differences from year to year. Therefore, if you are a Taurus born on April 20 or May 20, you'll find great clarity consulting a computer chart that tells you exactly where the Sun was at the very moment you were born.

*In a birth chart, a cusp is also the point at which an astrological House begins.

As for what span of time constitutes being born on the cusp, the astrological community holds various opinions. Some astrologers claim cusp means being born only within the first two days or last two days of a sign (though many say this is too narrow a time frame). Others say it can be as much as within the first ten days or last ten days of a sign (which many say is too wide an interpretation). The consensus is that you were born on the cusp if your birthday is within the first *five* days or last *five* days of a sign.

The question hanging over cusp-born people is: "What sign am I really?" They feel they straddle the border of two different countries. To some extent, this is true. If you were born on the cusp, you're under the influence of both signs. However, much like being a traveler leaving one country and crossing into another, you must actually *be* in one country—you can't be in two countries at the same time. One sign is always a stronger influence, and that sign is almost invariably the sign that the Sun was actually in (in other words, your Sun sign). The reason I say "almost" is that in rare cases a chart may be so heavily weighted with planets in a certain sign that the person more keenly feels the influence of that specific sign.

For example, I have a client who was born in the evening on May 20. On that evening, the Sun was leaving Taurus and entering Gemini. At the moment of his birth, the Sun was still in Taurus, so technically speaking, he is a Taurus. However, the Sun was only a couple hours away from being in Gemini, and this person has the Moon, Mercury, and Venus all in Gemini. He has always felt like a Gemini and has always behaved as a Gemini.

This, obviously, is an unusual case. Generally, the Sun is the most powerful planetary influence in a chart. Even if you were born with the Sun on the very tip of the first or last degree of Taurus, Taurus is your Sun sign—and this is the sign you will most feel like.

Still, the influence of the approaching sign or of the sign just ending is present, and you will probably sense that mixture in yourself.

BORN APRIL 20 THROUGH APRIL 24

You are Taurus with Aries tendencies. You are self-sufficient and determined, but also spirited and independent. You cannot bear being restricted by other people's rules, and whatever the situation, you always assert your own personality. People often come to you for advice; you may be known as having great style and confidence. In truth, you sometimes feel insecure, but you hide it very well. You firmly believe that your presentation of self is what colors others' perception of you. When confronting large tasks and complex projects, you take the intellectual approach. In love, however, you are impulsive and extravagant. In an affair, being wild and out of character appeals to your passionate heart, but in time (and through disappointment) you learn that romantic adventure *and* stability can successfully coexist.

BORN MAY 16 THROUGH MAY 20

You are Taurus with Gemini tendencies. You are ambitious, have strong willpower, and are also imaginative and intellectually inclined. You have a charismatic personality and possess a special persuasive touch that works well with people. Generally, you deal in a straightforward manner because you prefer to cut through deception or secretiveness and lay things out in the open. Also, your strong mental powers can clarify others' fuzzy thinking when you're trying to solve knotty problems. You have a pronounced streak of independence and dislike taking orders. Words come easily to you unless you are emotionally involved; then you are often unable to express your deepest feelings. This is especially true when you are in love—yet all one needs to read your emotions is notice how incredibly thoughtful your kind deeds are.

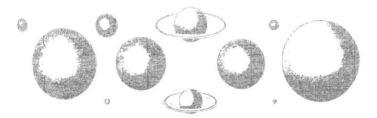

YOUR SPECIAL DAY OF BIRTH

APRIL 20

You're exciting and passionate, and can galvanize people. Your positive attitude is a precious gift you give to others. You attract success. In love, you're the lionhearted partner who's fiercely protective.

APRIL 21

You're an adventurer willing to go the extra mile—therefore you'll go farther than others. You have a powerhouse personality and a loving heart. Romantically, you're a sensuous lover.

APRIL 22

Your quick mind sets you apart. You're ambitious but also sensitive and caring. You try to create harmony, and are capable of loving deeply and forever. Be careful about becoming overly possessive.

APRIL 23

You're passionate about life and love, and have a dominating personality. You, however, see yourself as a pussycat. In your work, you're restless, and need independence.

APRIL 24

You are cultured, well-read, and a fascinating conversationalist. Though it's sometimes hard to penetrate your layer of reserved good manners, you're intensely sensitive.

APRIL 25

You have a presence that turns heads, and people feel honored to call you a friend. You will achieve your dreams because you're disciplined. In love, you're passionate and giving.

APRIL 26

Your feelings run deep. You bring intensity to everything you pursue. You're smart and dependable and also highly imaginative—a combination that spells ultimate triumph.

APRIL 27

Dynamic energies surround you. You're gregarious, inventive, and easily win over others. Your head rules your heart unless you're in love. Then you give your all.

APRIL 28

You're strong and tenacious and have the shoulder others lean on. You give your work your best effort, for you take failure very hard. In love, you are passionate and a truth teller.

APRIL 29

You're intuitive and a shrewd judge of character. But when you love someone, you're forgiving of all faults. Creatively, you're a dynamo blessed with superior intelligence.

APRIL 30

People are in awe of your accomplishments, yet you never feel the confidence others think you have. In love, you're a great romantic, and when you trust you're very sensual.

MAY 1

You're full of humor and also a calm presence in others' lives—a rare combination. In work, you're a pioneer. In love, you're truthful, honorable, and are promised happiness.

MAY 2

Your patience is legendary, which means you work hard at containing your volatile interior feelings. This strong control is evident in your career—and in love, your devotion runs deep.

MAY 3

With your gift for communicating and wacky sense of humor, you stand out as a star in your circle. You're also a prodigious worker and a flirt who believes in true love. You need a lover who matches your intelligence.

MAY 4

You have easy charm and an altruistic nature, but you're nobody's fool. Your sharp intellect and insight destine you to do unusual work. Love is chaotic until you meet your soulmate.

MAY 5

You like being a rebel yet also have a common touch that fits in with the mainstream. Success surrounds you. In love, you're sought after, though your heart chooses only one.

MAY 6

One of your great assets is your inquiring mind. You're analytical *and* creative, so you have a winning edge in both business and the arts. Romantically, you have a rich, deep fantasy life.

MAY 7

You demand perfection of yourself, so you are never satisfied. To others, however, you're a major achiever. In love, you yearn intensely, and ultimately will find the one who fills you.

MAY 8

You have originality and charm, and are a special favorite among your friends. In your work you're a stickler for detail but also have artistic imagination. In love, you're profoundly loyal.

MAY 9

You're a teacher and an actor with great ability to perform. You also enjoy snuggling up in your own home surrounded by family and friends. You're a *romantic* lover with an ability to create "movie moments."

MAY 10

You have street-smarts *and* high intellect (a "wow" combination)— and seem to draw creative ideas from a secret inner source. You're also a passionate sensualist who wants to plumb your lover's soul.

MAY 11

Others assume you attract success because of your buoyant attitude, but the truth is you're an extremely hard worker. Love brings out your best gifts of loyalty and cherishing, but you must learn not to sacrifice.

MAY 12

You're mischievous and funny, which, curiously, hides a serious approach to life. Your quality is to be emotional available. To your commitments you give 100 percent effort, and in love you offer your whole heart.

MAY 13

You're effective in public life, for you're good at influencing others. Your eclectic mind enjoys a wide range of subjects. Romantically, you can be elusive until you really fall hard.

MAY 14

You have intensity and energy, and with your innovative approach, you tend to break new ground in your work. It's hard to get to your secret emotional core, but the right lover can.

MAY 15

With your creative imagination, you're successful when you take *action* (rather than just dream). You're at your best in relationships, for you have a way of touching others' hearts.

MAY 16

You have flair and dynamism and spend much energy trying to tame your wildness. When you do, you're a prodigious accomplisher. Love does tend to be a soap opera, however.

MAY 17

You make everything you do look simple, but you go to immense effort others don't see. Inside, you also hide great depth of feeling and go out of your way to spoil your lover.

MAY 18

You have "incorruptibility"—people seek you out in business and friendship. In love, you're a steadfast partner who is deeply sensitive, and it takes a long time to recover from a hurt.

MAY 19

You are constantly learning and, at the same time, an accomplished achiever. Your zest for life energizes other people. Love gets complicated because you want freedom *and* commitment.

MAY 20

Your life is filled with unusual people and events. You're thought of as an "original," and are a gifted communicator. You may have to wait for true love to arrive.

YOU AND CHINESE ASTROLOGY

With Marco Polo's adventurous travels in A.D. 1275, Europeans learned for the first time of the great beauty, wealth, history, and romance of China. Untouched as they were by outside influences, the Chinese developed their astrology along different lines from other ancient cultures, such as the Egyptians, Babylonians, and Greeks from whom Western astrology has its roots. Therefore, the Chinese zodiac differs from the zodiac of the West. To begin with, it's based on a lunar cycle rather than Western astrology's solar cycle. The Chinese zodiac is divided into twelve years, and each year is represented by a different animal—the rat, ox, tiger, rabbit, dragon, snake, horse, goat, monkey, rooster, dog, and pig. The legend of the twelve animals is that when Buddha lay on his deathbed, he asked the animals of the forest to come and bid him farewell. These twelve were the first to arrive. The cat, as the story goes, is not among the animals because it was napping and couldn't be bothered to make the journey. (In some Asian countries, such as Vietnam, the cat replaces the rabbit.)

Like Western astrology, in which the zodiac signs have different characteristics, each of the twelve Chinese animal years assigns character traits specific to a person born in that year. For example, the Year of the Rat confers honesty and an analytical mind, whereas the Year of the Monkey grants charm and quick ability to spot opportunity.

Here are descriptions for Taurus for each Chinese animal year:

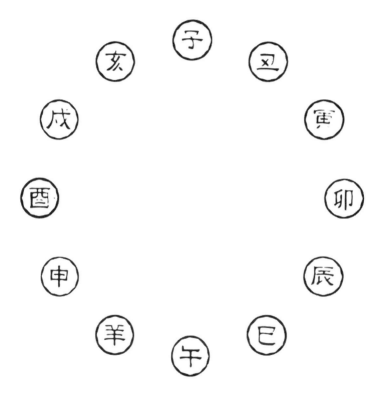

IF YOU ARE TAURUS BORN IN THE YEAR OF THE RAT

Years of the Rat

1900	1960	2020	2080
1912	1972	2032	2092
1924	1984	2044	
1936	1996	2056	
1948	2008	2068	

The Rat is courageous, clever, and charismatic—and also nervous and meddling. Your Taurus elegance and the grace with which you handle people combine with the Rat's intelligence to make you super successful in the public arena. You're very smart and love to be engaged in projects that challenge your mind. Rats have an ability to stash away for the future, and this definitely notches up your Taurus propensity for amassing and collecting wealth, security, friends, and beautiful possessions. Your tendency to feel unsafe when you don't have enough of what you want is heightened by the Rat's worrywart inclinations. In love, you are capable of great sacrifice for those you care for. Just be careful not to stay in the wrong relationship because you're anxious about the future. Compatible partners are born in the Years of the Monkey, Pig, Rat, and Snake.

IF YOU ARE TAURUS BORN IN THE YEAR OF THE OX

Years of the Ox

1901	1961	2021	2081
1913	1973	2033	2093
1925	1985	2045	
1937	1997	2057	
1949	2009	2069	

Natives of the Year of the Ox are said to be good-natured, indus-trious, capable, purposeful, stubborn, and inflexible. Don't these sound like Taurus qualities? How interesting that the Chinese Ox and the Taurus Bull have so much in common—just as the actual animals are so much alike. Your Taurus practicality and the orderly way you think blend well with the Ox's calm, methodical approach. As a Taurus Ox, you immediately gain the confidence and support of others. You're an inspiring leader—although your legendary stubbornness is twice as strong. Eloquence, too, is an Ox characteristic and, added to your Taurus warmth and tender heart, confers an ability to express feelings and be an excellent writer. In love, you are deeply committed and deeply sensual. Compatible partners are born in the Years of the Rabbit, Rooster, Monkey, Pig, and Snake.

IF YOU ARE TAURUS BORN IN THE YEAR OF THE TIGER

Years of the Tiger

1902	1962	2022	2082
1914	1974	2034	2094
1926	1986	2046	
1938	1998	2058	
1950	2010	2070	

Tiger natives are born with magnetism. To Buddhists, the Tiger symbolizes the power of faith, and the Chinese believe that the Year of the Tiger bestows great gifts of intelligence, charisma, and extra luck. Certainly, the pride and strength of the Tiger meld beautifully with the perseverance and practicality of Taurus. As a Taurus Tiger, you're well suited for positions of responsibility. Your creative talents, business sense, and personal style dominate the scene. You impress people without even trying. Those born in the Year of the Tiger are said to be passionate and possessive, traits underscored by your fierce Taurean loyalty and search for security within relationships. In love, you tend to be overprotective and exhibit a jealous streak. Compatible partners are born in the Years of the Rabbit, Dog, Dragon, Monkey, Pig, and Tiger.

IF YOU ARE TAURUS BORN IN THE YEAR OF THE RABBIT

Years of the Rabbit

1903	1963	2023	2083
1915	1975	2035	2095
1927	1987	2047	
1939	1999	2059	
1951	2011	2071	

The Chinese imbue the Rabbit with qualities of refinement, sociability, and rich imagination. As a Taurus Rabbit, therefore, you are extra creative and have a theatrical aura that comes naturally. All Taureans have personal flair, but your ability to hold an audience's attention is especially pronounced. You're particularly successful in work in which you have to deal with the public. Being born in the Year of the Rabbit endows you with an active mind interested in the world at large, and this combined with your Taurus fondness for the finer things of life makes you an arbiter of taste in your crowd. You have a gift for attracting attention—and in love, you are a romantic "seducer" who entices and enchants, and keeps romance alive. Compatible partners are born in the Years of the Goat, Dog, Dragon, Snake, Horse, and Monkey.

IF YOU ARE TAURUS BORN IN THE YEAR OF THE DRAGON

辰

Years of the Dragon

1904	1964	2024	2084
1916	1976	2036	2096
1928	1988	2048	
1940	2000	2060	
1952	2012	2072	

The Dragon is special, for in Asia it symbolizes life force, luck, abundance, and immortality. People born in the Year of the Dragon are said to have the persistence and willpower to realize their ideals, qualities that are also very Taurean. The Dragon and Taurus align harmoniously. As a Dragon, you're outspoken and totally incapable of meanness. Your loyalty and honesty are renowned. Add all this to your Taurus charisma, devoted determination, and talented artistic eye, and you can see you're doubly blessed with fascinating *attractiveness*. People are drawn to your strength of will and your generous heart—your unusual combination of power and softness. In love, you're a total giver, and are particularly sensual and seductive. The only downside is your possessiveness. Compatible partners are born in the Years of the Rabbit, Goat, Monkey, Snake, and Tiger.

IF YOU ARE TAURUS BORN IN THE YEAR OF THE SNAKE

Years of the Snake

1905	1965	2025	2085
1917	1977	2037	2097
1929	1989	2049	
1941	2001	2061	
1953	2013	2073	

Contrary to how the Snake is viewed in the West, in Asian mythology it is a creature of benevolence and aesthetic beauty. Those born in the Year of the Snake are said to be well bred, cultivated, and cerebral. The Snake year confers elegance and fluidity of speech that, combined with your Taurus brainpower and sociability, blesses you with a charismatic allure. You're known for your humor and charm. You also have a strong independent streak. All Taureans determinedly carve out their own special bailiwick, but as a Taurus Snake you particularly won't run with the pack. You have an intuition or clairvoyance about what will be successful, and you follow that path. In love, you're intense. You have great power to attract, and your romantic life can get chaotic. Compatible partners are born in the Years of the Rabbit, Rooster, Dragon, Horse, Ox, and Rat.

IF YOU ARE TAURUS BORN IN THE YEAR OF THE HORSE

Years of the Horse

1906	1966	2026	2086
1918	1978	2038	2098
1930	1990	2050	
1942	2002	2062	
1954	2014	2074	

In the Asian world, the Horse is a shining star, symbol of freedom and a passion for life. The Year of the Horse lends an extroverted gaiety and a spirit of rebellion—or at least an inclination to march to a different drummer. Those born in a Horse year are said to choose unconventional careers, move to distant places, and be driven by a need to experience a larger-than-life life. This exploratory bent combined with your Taurus determination and ambition creates a powerhouse personality. As a Taurus Horse, you're capable of high achievement. You stand out because you make the success you attain seem so effortless. In romantic relationships, you're ardent, sentimental, highly sensual, and can fall in love at first sight. Compatible partners are born in the Years of the Rabbit, Rooster, Goat, Horse, and Snake.

IF YOU ARE TAURUS BORN IN THE YEAR OF THE GOAT

Years of the Goat

1907	1967	2027	2087
1919	1979	2039	2099
1931	1991	2051	
1943	2003	2063	
1955	2015	2075	

To the Chinese, the Goat represents the dreamer and muse. People born in the Year of the Goat are said to be highly creative and thrive in the fertile fields of imagination. Goat natives are inventive and intelligent and full of whimsy. The Year of the Goat also confers perseverance and stick-to-it-iveness—which, come to think of it, is very much like your Taurus combination of an artistic, elegant style with a patient, determined approach. Goat and Taurus energies blend beautifully, and you're capable of putting forth yeoman effort that gleans huge results. In the end, you will get what you need—security. Romantically, you're amorous and sexually generous, willing to go to great lengths to please your lover. Compatible partners are born in the Years of the Rabbit, Dragon, Horse, Monkey, and Pig.

IF YOU ARE TAURUS BORN IN THE YEAR OF THE MONKEY

Years of the Monkey

1908	1968	2028	2088
1920	1980	2040	2100
1932	1992	2052	
1944	2004	2064	
1956	2016	2076	

Monkey people are said to be curious, playful, and intelligent—but with something more. The Chinese believe those born in the Year of the Monkey are destined to live lives that are considered glamorous and exotic—for example, achieving fame in the creative arts or becoming a guru-type leader. Add this to your Taurus drive and tenacity, and you can't help but be a mover and shaker in whatever field you choose. As a Taurus Monkey, you're known for your remarkable brainpower (you're a storehouse of facts and ideas) and ability to spot business opportunity. The Monkey's jolly public persona makes your Taurus charm even more endearing. In romance, you're flirtatious and sensuous and, unless you're deeply in love, can be somewhat of a rover. Compatible partners are born in the Years of the Rabbit, Dragon, Ox, Pig, Rat, and Tiger.

IF YOU ARE TAURUS BORN IN THE YEAR OF THE ROOSTER

Years of the Rooster

1909	1957	2005	2053
1921	1969	2017	2065
1933	1981	2029	2077
1945	1993	2041	2089

The Rooster symbolizes courage—in Japanese mythology, the Rooster is dedicated to the Goddess of the Sun for rescuing her. People born in the Year of the Rooster are said to be sincere, enthusiastic, successful with people, and outspoken. Indeed, candor and honesty are striking characteristics, as is having captivating style. These attributes combined with your Taurus strength of purpose give you a "ruling class" charisma. Others see you as brilliant and compelling; you have a special radiance. You're well suited for adventurous projects, for when you get an idea in your head, you won't be dissuaded. In love, you are faithful, with deep, straight-from-the-heart loyalty, though you need to learn when to let go. As a Taurus Rooster, you have double fixity. Compatible partners are born in the Years of the Horse, Ox, and Snake.

IF YOU ARE TAURUS BORN IN THE YEAR OF THE DOG

Years of the Dog

1910	1958	2006	2054
1922	1970	2018	2066
1934	1982	2030	2078
1946	1994	2042	2090

In China, the Dog symbolizes a crusading spirit—the energy to make the world a better place. Just like the real-life animal, the Asian astrological Dog is faithful, honest, loyal, and devoted. Those born in the Year of the Dog are said to be heroic—they keep their promises and can be counted on in any situation. These qualities give your Taurus commitment an extra dimension, for as a Taurus Dog you dedicate yourself to a mission. This may be on a personal level (e.g., the happiness of your lover or welfare of your family), or on a wider scale in political or social action. You're also excellent at detail work. In love, you're sentimental, tender, and deeply giving (even sacrificial)—but your possessiveness can bring you heartache. Compatible partners are born in the Years of the Rabbit, Dog, Pig, and Tiger.

IF YOU ARE TAURUS BORN IN THE YEAR OF THE PIG

Years of the Pig

1911	1959	2007	2055
1923	1971	2019	2067
1935	1983	2031	2079
1947	1995	2043	2091

In contrast to the West's derisive attitude, the Chinese view the astrological Pig as chivalrous and gallant. The Pig symbolizes warmth, abundance, sweetness, and purity of heart. Those born in the Year of the Pig are said to be loving, peaceable, and scrupulous in their dealings. These qualities combine seamlessly with Taurus's generous nature and willingness to go the distance—you're totally trustworthy in all your commitments, personal and professional. Taurus Pigs are wise leaders who make others feel protected. You're also an ardent seeker of knowledge with cosmopolitan taste and style—a voluptuary who enjoys good food and luxurious surroundings. Likewise, in love you're a sensualist but never promiscuous. You devote your whole heart to the one you love. Compatible partners are born in the Years of the Rabbit, Dog, Pig, and Tiger.

YOU AND NUMEROLOGY

Numerology is the language of numbers. It is the belief that there is a correlation between numbers and living things, ideas, and concepts. Certainly, numbers surround and infuse our lives (e.g., twenty-four hours in a day, twelve months of the year, etc.). And from ancient times mystics have taught that numbers carry a *vibration*, a deeper meaning that defines how each of us fits into the universe. According to numerology, you are born with a personal number that contains information about who you are and what you need to be happy. This number expresses what numerology calls your life path.

All numbers reduce to one of nine digits, numbers 1 through 9. Your personal number is based on your date of birth. To calculate your number, write your birth date in numerals. As an example, the birth date of April 29, 1985, is written 4-29-1985. Now begin the addition: 4 + 29 + 1 + 9 + 8 + 5 = 56; 56 reduces to 5 + 6 = 11; 11 reduces to 1 + 1 = 2. The personal number for someone born April 29, 1985, is *Two*.

IF YOU ARE A TAURUS ONE

Keywords: Confidence and Creativity

One is the number of leadership and new beginnings. You're courageous and inventive, and people respond to your decisiveness if not always to your edgy impatience. You're attracted to unusual creative pursuits because you like to be one-of-a-kind. You can't bear to be under the thumb of other people's whims and agendas. Careers that call to you are those in which you carve out your own area of expertise and you're in charge. As for love, you want ecstasy and passion, and you thrill to the excitement of a beginning affair. However, in spite of your flirtatious eye, you will truly fall in love with someone with whom you feel you have "come home."

IF YOU ARE A TAURUS TWO

Keywords: Cooperation and Balance

Two is the number of cooperation and creating a secure entity. Being a Two gives you extra Taurus magnetism—you attract what you need. Perhaps you're a collector of esthetic objects, and certainly you hold relationships close. Your magic is not only your people skills, but also your ability to breathe life into empty forms (e.g., a concept, an ambitious business idea, a new relationship) and produce something of worth. You're a perfectionist in your work. With determination and persistence, you attain material things. In love, you are deeply sensual and sexual. Your desire is for a loving partnership with someone you can trust and share confidences with.

IF YOU ARE A TAURUS THREE

Keywords: Expression and Sensitivity

Three symbolizes self-expression. You have a joyful personality, a gift for words, and a talent for visualization. Creativity and innovation are your specialties. You're a quick study and a quick wit—versatile, sociable, mentally active. Happily, you have good financial timing. You also have Taurus commitment and always follow through on your word. People see you as an honorable leader and a good friend. In love you need someone who excites you intellectually and sensually, and understands your complex personality. Casual acquaintances may not see your depth, but in love you must have a soulmate who does.

IF YOU ARE A TAURUS FOUR

Keywords: Stability and Process

Four is the number of dedication and loyalty. It represents *foundation*, exactly as a four-sided square does. Being a Four intensifies your Taurus ability to build. First you plan, then day-by-day you add the next step, the next layer, keeping on schedule. You create Taurus stability by following a process, and your strength is that you're persistent. Therefore, you're able to control your environment, accomplish great works, and achieve high honor. In love, you adore closeness and being enclosed in a downy quilt of security. You look for a relationship with staying power. You need a faithful, giving, and understanding lover.

IF YOU ARE A TAURUS FIVE

Keywords: Freedom and Discipline

Five is the number of change and freedom. Unlike many Taureans, you enjoy exploring innovative ideas. With your chameleon intellect (it can go in any direction) and captivating ability to deal with people, you're a marvelous *persuader*. You charm and influence others, and have great skill with the public. In career, your specialty is to make something you love an extension of you (a creative project, for example), so that the work becomes *your* style. In love, you need romantic fantasy but also want a partner who looks ahead to new goals. When you give your heart away it's to someone with whom you passionately mesh—body and mind.

IF YOU ARE A TAURUS SIX

Keywords: Vision and Acceptance

Six is the number of teaching, healing, and utilizing your talents. You were born with idealism, and love really does rule your universe. But your life is not just sweetness and light. You're competitive, exacting, and demanding—especially with yourself. You use your sharp intellect to improve any situation you're in. Responsibility is not a burden, but a gateway to finding your true purpose. Achieving high goals fills you with happiness. You'd like life to run like a well-oiled machine; you're a *perfector*. In love, you're fervent about being a helpmate as well as a lover. You're also a secret sensualist who gives your all to someone you trust.

IF YOU ARE A TAURUS SEVEN

Keywords: Trust and Openness

Seven is the number of the mystic and the intensely focused specialist. You have an instinct for problem-solving, and in a flash understand how things work (in business, between people, etc.). You're an intellectual, a philosopher, and connoisseur of everything creative. Because you're a questioner and thinker, in your work you're determined to get to the heart of whatever the puzzle is. Of course you seek stability, but unlike many Taureans you're able to stir things up and get out of an old trap. At your core you're extremely loving, though very selective about relationships. Your deepest need is for a love partner who can help you in your journey to becoming the real you.

IF YOU ARE A TAURUS EIGHT

Keywords: Abundance and Power

Eight is the number of mastery and authority. You are intelligent, alert, quick in action, born to take power in your own hands and guide traffic into the direction you want. Others sense you're the one who knows best, and they're right. You think big, tackle the hard stuff, and never let anyone down. Your values include being truthful, honest, and getting results. Taurus is the sign of abundance and, as an Eight, you have a passion for enlargement— which may include reaching out to diversified groups and adding to your education. You are a protective and deeply caring lover, and in turn you need to know your lover is your unwavering ally.

IF YOU ARE A TAURUS NINE

Keywords: Integrity and Wisdom

Nine is the path of the "old soul," the number of completion and full bloom. Because it's the last number, it sums up the highs and lows of human experience, and you live a life of dramatic events. You're very intellectual, deeply feeling, extremely protective, interested in all kinds of exploration. People see you as colorful and heroic because you have an adventurous outlook but are also spiritual and altruistic. Your quest is to channel your energy into what is captivating, worthwhile, and lasting. You're a great romantic and highly sensual creature. In love, you give your all, often to the point of being sacrificing.

LAST WORD: YOUR TAURUS UNFINISHED BUSINESS

Psychologists often use the phrase *unfinished business* to describe unresolved issues—for example, patterns from childhood that cause unhappiness, anger that keeps one stuck, scenarios of family dysfunction that repeat through second and third generations (such as alcoholism or abusive behavior).

Astrology teaches that the past is indeed very much with us in the present—and that using astrological insights can help us to move out of emotional darkness into greater clarity. Even within this book (which is not a tome of hundreds of pages) you have read of many of the superlatives and challenges of being Taurus. You have breathtaking gifts and at the same time certain tendencies that can undermine utilizing these abilities.

In nature, a fascinating fact is that in jungles and forests a poisonous plant will grow in a certain spot, and always just a few feet away is a plant that's the antidote to that specific poison. Likewise, in astrology, the antidote is right there, ready to be used when the negatives threaten to overwhelm your life.

Taurus's unfinished business centers on inflexibility. The Taurean closed-mind cuts off possibility. You're antithetical to views that you don't hold. You have rigid rules, and others must toe the line. Taurus's focus on materialism results in being status-conscious and how you look to other people—how your home, your car, your clothes look. By the same token you tend to judge others by their exterior (are they well off, well dressed?) and turn a blind eye to a person's deeper self. You can be narrow-minded about odd things (food, for example, or what you deem "appropriate"). Taurus lives life as if it were a mapped-out plan, and deviating from the map means you've lost your way. More often than not you say no to taking side paths. Logically, you understand the need for change, but then you refuse to budge.

Inertia, too, keeps you rooted and bound. Unwilling to move out of your comfort zone, you'll put up with situations others would flee from. The sullen tolerance of Taurus reduces to apathy, and there you are, imprisoned by what you've allowed to enclose you.

Yet the antidotes are there, to be found in their entirety in being Taurus. No one has fiercer determination—which is the positive side of your obstinacy. When confronted by a project you've committed to, you drive yourself until it's done. You can be *counted* on, one of the rarest qualities in a culture filled with the unreliable and unstable.

Another antidote is your astonishing creativity. Your world is filled with color, design, beauty—you see this in your mind's eye. Instantly, you're able to bring harmony into your environment, into all the ordinary, everyday objects and settings around you. Your appreciation for the arts (music, painting, decoration, writing) is a source of joy, a renewable resource.

Also, your Taurus unfinished business is everything you're still on the way to accomplish. Remember, you're the sign of *value*. Being a Taurus means learning to value yourself and what you do. When you are true to yourself, you cannot help but be authentic with everyone else. Your task is to preserve what is valuable from the past and, holding these treasures, be able to move into the next adventure that will add to your personal "estate."

The essence of life is change—it will change no matter what we do and don't do. Once you push past your fear (which is what keeps you clinging to the deadening familiar), you begin to be truly alive. Astrology teaches that the journey of Taurus is to find your *heart*. The heart can turn inward and close off, or it can look outward to embrace relationships and meaningful work. You can utilize the strength of character that is your Taurus birthright—to build security, find creative freedom, and discover the richness of enduring love. All this is your unfinished business.

FAMOUS PEOPLE WITH THE SUN IN TAURUS

Akon
Ann-Margret
Fred Astaire
Mary Astor
Burt Bacharach
Stephen Baldwin
Lionel Barrymore
Candice Bergen
Irving Berlin
Yogi Berra
Cate Blanchett
Johannes Brahms
Carol Burnett
George Carlin
Cher
George Clooney
Stephen Colbert
Perry Como
Gary Cooper
Bing Crosby
Kirsten Dunst
Albert Finney
Ella Fitzgerald
Henry Fonda
Sigmund Freud
Martha Graham
Ulysses S. Grant

Orson Welles
William Randolph Hearst
Joseph Heller
Audrey Hepburn
Katharine Hepburn
Glenda Jackson
Janet Jackson
Reggie Jackson
Bianca Jagger
Jasper Johns
Dwayne "The Rock" Johnson
Grace Jones
Harper Lee
Jay Leno
Sugar Ray Leonard
Leonardo da Vinci
Liberace
Anita Loos
Joe Louis
Karl Marx
Rod McKuen
Shirley MacLaine
Bernard Malamud
Tim McGraw
Gold Meir
Yehudi Menuhin
Patrice Munsel

Vladimir Nabokov
Willie Nelson
Jack Nicholson
Florence Nightingale
Ryan O'Neal
Al Pacino
Eva Perón
Roberta Peters
Michelle Pfeiffer
Ezio Pinza
Pope John Paul II
Sergei Prokofiev
Anthony Quinn
Bertrand Russell
Pete Seeger
Jerry Seinfeld
William Shakespeare
Benjamin Spock
James Stewart
Barbra Streisand
Peter Ilyich Tchaikovsky
Shirley Temple
Uma Therman
Harry S. Truman
Rudolph Valentino

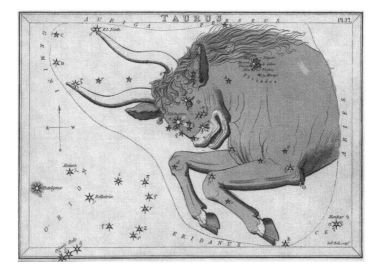

PART TWO

ALL ABOUT YOUR SIGN OF TAURUS

TAURUS'S ASTROLOGICAL AFFINITIES, LINKS, AND LORE

SYMBOL: The Bull 🐃

Strong, stubborn, plodding, can be both fierce and gentle. Despite being the epitome of male power, historically the Bull is aligned with female energy and represents the earth mother. The Bull symbolizes fertility and the renewal of life in springtime.

RULING PLANET: Venus ♀

Roman goddess of pleasure, beauty, adornment, the arts, love, sensuality, and harmonious relationships. In Latin, the word *Venus* means love and sexual desire. The Roman goddess Venus was the Greek goddess Aphrodite who ruled over flowers and gardens as well as seduction and enticement. Astrologically, Venus's influence inclines toward a love of luxury, exceptional creative ability, a gift for nurturing, and charming sociability. Venus is linked to the capacity to express affection and enjoy beauty.

DOMINANT KEYWORD

I HAVE

GLYPH ♉

The pictograph represents the horns and head of the Bull or Mother Cow (which, in ancient civilizations was the symbol for the nurturing Mother Earth). It also outlines the chin and Adam's apple of the human throat (the part of the anatomy that Taurus rules). In symbolic terms, the glyph is a half-moon forming a cup that rests on the circle of the Sun. The cup represents material power and wealth derived through the force of will (the circle).

PART OF THE BODY RULED BY TAURUS:
Neck and Throat

Many Taurus people have beautiful speaking and singing voices, but as a native of this sign, you're vulnerable to colds, laryngitis, sore throats, and thyroid problems.

LUCKY DAY: Friday

The day named for Venus, ruler of Taurus. Friday comes from the Old English *frigedaeg* (Day of Frige), which was a translation from the Latin for Day of Venus. This day is said to bring passion and harmony into your life.

LUCKY NUMBERS: 6 and 4

Numerologically, 6 represents teaching and nurturing, and 4 is linked to stability and dedication. These qualities align with the nature of Taurus.

TAROT CARD: The Hierophant

The card in the Tarot linked to Taurus is the Hierophant. Ancient names for this card are the High Priest and the Magus of the Eternal. In the Tarot, this card signifies intelligence, wisdom, and good counsel. It speaks of adhering to right principles, and through responsible action discovering deeper meaning in life. The Hierophant points to knowledge you already have in your heart. When this card turns up in a Tarot reading, it tells you to follow the ethical rules and fit in as a contributing member of your group.

The card itself pictures a spiritual leader (a pope or esoteric master) wearing the crown of a pope and seated on a throne between two pillars. He holds a scepter with a triple cross, and two crossed keys are at his feet. The seated figure represents wise teaching, the pillars are the duality between the material and the mystical, the scepter is discipline, and the crossed keys are keys to the kingdom of the spiritual.

For Taurus, the Hierophant says you always have a sense of the right thing to do, that with kindness and integrity you are in a state of wholeness and live a divinely ordered life.

MAGICAL BIRTHSTONE: Emerald

One of the most precious of all stones that from ancient times has been given magical status. The word *emerald* means "green" and "shine." In Egyptian mythology the God of Knowledge wrote on an emerald tablet, and thus the gem signified wisdom. Emeralds were placed on Egyptian mummies to give them vigor on their journey to the next life, for green symbolized renewal. Associated with love, fertility, and creative imagination, the emerald was among the Roman goddess Venus's favorite gemstones. In many modern cultures travelers carry an emerald as a protective talisman and lovers give the stone as token of commitment. For Taurus, the emerald is said to protect against infidelity and deceit, ensure loyalty, and improve memory.

SPECIAL COLORS: Pale Blue and Mauve

The soft colors of refinement and gentleness. These colors signify loyalty, intelligence, and high ethics. Pale blue especially denotes contemplation, and mauve is the color of patience.

CONSTELLATION OF TAURUS

Science dates the naming of the Taurus constellation back to the Copper Age in approximately 4000 B.C. It's believed this was the first constellation to which human beings gave a name, and they assigned this star-grouping to the deity of the Bull. In Greek mythology the god Zeus often took the form of a white bull. Classically, the Bull symbolized power, strength, richness, and fertility. In addition, 6,000 years ago, the Spring Equinox took place in this constellation—thus Taurus is linked to the concept of the fruitfulness of Mother Earth. The brightest star in the Taurus constellation is Aldebaran, called the Heart of the Bull. One of this constellation's ancient names was *Te*, meaning "foundation."

CITIES

Dublin, Lucerne, Leipzig, St. Louis

COUNTRIES

Ireland, Switzerland, Cyprus, Greece

FLOWERS

Violet and Poppy

TREES

Cypress and Apple. In mythology, both trees represented fertility.

HERBS AND SPICES

Cloves, Sorrel, Spearmint

METAL: Copper

A malleable metal prized for its beautiful color and thermal conductivity. Copper has been in use for over 10,000 years. This metal was sacred to the goddess Venus, and the written symbol for copper and for the planet Venus (ruler of Taurus) is the same. In the ancient world, copper fashioned into lightning rods was used as protection against lightning, and therefore considered a guard against all evil influences. Egyptians placed copper behind the heads of mummies to provide "warmth" on their journey to the afterlife. Copper is also considered to have healing powers; even today copper bracelets are worn as an antidote to the aches and pains of arthritis and rheumatism.

ANIMALS RULED BY TAURUS

Cattle

DANGER

Taurus people have a tendency to get involved in violent situations that have to do with love or money. They often antagonize others and incite the passions of lovers because of their stubbornness and possessiveness.

PERSONAL PROVERB

The price of greatness is responsibility.

KEYWORDS FOR TAURUS

Strong willed

Reliable

Determined

Ambitious

Stubborn

Dogmatic

Practical

Loyal

Fond of the familiar and resistant to change

Creative

A love of beauty and luxury

Affectionate

Romantic

Sensual

Passionate

Needing close attachments

Nurturing

Possessive and jealous

Clever in business and finances

Talent for gathering worldly goods

Managerial and having the ability to organize

An eye for value and what will gain in worth

HOW ASTROLOGY SLICES AND DICES YOUR SIGN OF TAURUS

DUALITY: Feminine

The twelve astrological signs are divided into two groups, *masculine* and *feminine*. Six are masculine and six are feminine; this is known as the sign's *duality*. A masculine sign is direct and energetic. A feminine sign is receptive and magnetic. These attributes were given to the signs about 2,500 years ago. Today modern astrologers avoid the sexism implicit in these distinctions. A masculine sign does not mean "positive and forceful" any more than a feminine sign means "negative and weak." In modern terminology, the masculine signs are defined as outer-directed and strong through action. The feminine signs, such as your sign of Taurus, are self-contained and strong through inner reserves.

TRIPLICITY (ELEMENT): Earth

The twelve signs are also divided into groups of three signs each. These three-sign groups are called a *triplicity*, and each of these denotes an *element*. The elements are *Fire*, *Earth*, *Air*, and *Water*. In astrology, an element symbolizes a fundamental characterization of the sign.

The three *Fire* signs are Aries, Leo, and Sagittarius. Fire signs are active and enthusiastic.

The three *Earth* signs are Taurus, Virgo, and Capricorn. Earth signs are practical and stable.

The three *Air* signs are Gemini, Libra, and Aquarius. Air signs are intellectual and communicative.

The three *Water* signs are Cancer, Scorpio, and Pisces. Water signs are emotional and intuitive.

QUADRUPLICITY (QUALITY): Fixed

The twelve signs are also divided into groups of four signs each. These four-sign groups are called a *quadruplicity*, and each of these denotes a *quality*. The qualities are *Cardinal*, *Fixed*, and *Mutable*. In astrology, the quality signifies the sign's interaction with the outside world.

Four signs are *Cardinal** signs. They are Aries, Cancer, Libra, and Capricorn. Cardinal signs are enterprising and outgoing. They are the initiators.

Four signs are *Fixed*. They are Taurus, Leo, Scorpio, and Aquarius. Fixed signs are resistant to change. They are perfectors and finishers rather than originators.

Four signs are *Mutable*. They are Gemini, Virgo, Sagittarius, and Pisces. Mutable signs are flexible, versatile, and adaptable. They are able to adjust to differing circumstances.

*When the Sun crosses the four cardinal points in the zodiac, we mark the beginning of each of our four seasons. Aries begins spring; Cancer begins summer; Libra begins fall; Capricorn begins winter.

Your sign of Taurus is a Feminine, Earth, Fixed sign—and no other sign in the zodiac is this exact combination. Your sign is a one-of-a-kind combination, and therefore you express the characteristics of your duality, element, and quality differently from any other sign.

For example, your sign is a *Feminine* sign, meaning you are receptive, caring, resourceful. You're an *Earth* sign, meaning you're enduring, practical, and stable. And you're a *Fixed* sign, meaning you're dedicated, committed, resistant to change, in for the long haul.

Now, the sign of Virgo is also Feminine and Earth, but unlike Taurus (which is Fixed), Virgo is Mutable. Therefore, like you, Virgo is giving, nurturing, and a perfector. You both share a practical approach and commitment to giving your best effort. However, being Mutable, Virgo is changeable. It tends to have many irons in the fire and scatter its energy. Virgo can be sidetracked (especially by its fussy perfectionism) and lose sight of the big picture. You, on the other hand, are Fixed, and your overriding quality is stick-to-it-iveness. You're not distracted by a confusing variety of choices. You lay the foundations and patiently keep creating.

Capricorn, too, is Feminine and Earth, but unlike Taurus (which is Fixed) Capricorn is Cardinal. Capricorn, like you, is a creative achiever with great powers of commitment. But being Cardinal, Capricorn needs to stir up changes (sometimes unnecessarily) and be viewed by others as a mover and shaker. Capricorn wants to be the authority; if in its opinion a job at hand is too mundane or unimportant, Capricorn will abandon it in search of a star-making project. Concerned with the face it shows to the world, Capricorn wants glory and to be the pacesetter. You, being Fixed, have the power of completion. You will out-endure any obstacle or competition, and your patience is legendary. When you choose to commit (whether to work or a relationship), you do so because you value what you give yourself to. Therefore, you are unswayed in your dedication.

POLARITY: Scorpio

The twelve signs are also divided into groups of two signs each. These two-sign groups are called a *polarity* (meaning "opposite"). Each sign in the zodiac has a polarity, which is its opposite sign in the other half of the zodiac. The two signs express opposite characteristics.

Taurus and Scorpio are a polarity. Taurus is the sign of money, possessions, property, and material gain. Taurus puts high regard on valuable possessions, not only for their intrinsic worth, but for their aesthetic beauty. Indeed the theme of *ownership* runs through your character. You're attached to the people and things you cherish—you hold on to the objects you lovingly collect and cling to the relationships you treasure. Taurus also focuses on building up financial affluence, for wealth and goods create a feeling of a stable universe. Of course, being Venus-ruled, you also enjoy the esthetics of a prosperous life—such as owning elegant possessions and enjoying pastimes such as theater and fine dining. You're also very creative in such areas as crafts, writing, music, decorating, and designing.

As a Taurus, your psychological agenda is to gather in and keep. You're an Earth sign, and astrology speaks of you being rooted in the things of the earth (such as money, food, real estate) as well as being down-to-earth and practical. You're an extraordinary combination of realism and artistry.

Scorpio, your opposite sign, is the sign of legacies, shared wealth, inheritance, and gain from the past. The wealth of Scorpio people is often spiritual rather than material, which they give to others in the form of teaching and the healing arts. Scorpio rules endings that lead to new beginnings, exploration of the unknown, emotional depth, and profound sexuality. Its realm is the hidden, what lies beneath the surface.

Interestingly, a Taurus person is sometimes mistaken for a Scorpio, and vice versa, because these two signs have much in common. Both of you are persistent, unwavering, intense in your commitments and need for security. But Scorpio is a Water sign, and its domain is the emotional—intuition, perception, will, inner yearning, memory, passion. Scorpio channels emotional energy into getting its goals, but its drive is less for things than for knowledge and control. It craves power over every aspect of its environment. Scorpio is the behind-the-scenes mastermind, whereas Taurus is the hands-on builder.